Come On In

This guest book belongs to

_____

_____

_____

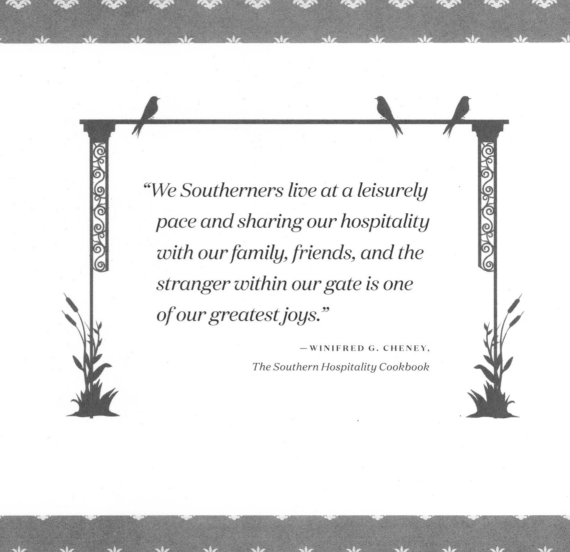

"We Southerners live at a leisurely pace and sharing our hospitality with our family, friends, and the stranger within our gate is one of our greatest joys."

—WINIFRED G. CHENEY,
The Southern Hospitality Cookbook

"I've learned that people will forget what you said, people will forget what you did, but people will never forget how you made them feel."

MAYA ANGELOU

"There is nothing like Southern hospitality. It's such a beautiful and genuine thing."

—ABIGAIL SPENCER

"It was a good moment, the kind you would like to press between the pages of a book, or hide in your sock drawer, so you could touch it again."

— RICK BRAGG,
All Over but the Shoutin'

"There's something timeless and important about making people laugh, about being the right spot in their day."

— REESE WITHERSPOON

"Love grows from stable relationships, shared experience, loyalty, devotion, trust."

—RICHARD WRIGHT,
Native Son

"Food imaginatively and lovingly prepared, and eaten in good company, warms the being with something more than the mere intake of calories. I cannot conceive of cooking for friends or family, under reasonable conditions, as being a chore."

— MARJORIE KINNAN RAWLINGS

"Our most treasured family heirloom are our sweet family memories."

—WILLIAM
FAULKNER

"*If you are Southern, you never run out of company.*"

—ALFRE WOODARD

"Always believe in things
and people that bring you
pleasure. What good does
it do to throw those things
out the window?"

—PAT CONROY,
The Great Santini

"Good friends, good books, and a sleepy conscience: this is the ideal life."

MARK TWAIN

"I don't believe that blood makes a family; kin is the circle you create, hands held tight."

—TAYARI JONES,
An American Marriage

"Life is partly what we make it, and partly what it is made with the friends we choose."

TENNESSEE WILLIAMS

All rights reserved.
Published in the United States by Clarkson Potter/Publishers,
an imprint of Random House, a division of
Penguin Random House LLC, New York.
clarksonpotter.com

CLARKSON POTTER is a trademark and POTTER with colophon
is a registered trademark of Penguin Random House LLC.

ISBN 978-1-9848-2609-1

Printed in China

Cover and interior illustrations by Jennifer Heuer
Cover design by Ian Dingman
Interior design by Marysarah Quinn

10 9 8 7 6 5 4 3 2 1

First Edition